BURIAL SERVICE

OF THE

Orders of Knighthood

AS ADOPTED BY THE

GRAND COMMANDERY OF MICHIGAN,

AND RECOMMENDED BY THE

GRAND ENCAMPMENT OF KNIGHTS TEMPLAR OF THE UNITED STATES.

Printed for use of Detroit Commandery, K. T., No. 1.

DETROIT:
THE DAILY POST PRINTING ESTABLISHMENT.
1868.

IHS

GENERAL REGULATIONS.

1. No Sir Knight can be buried with the funeral honors of Knighthood, unless he be a Knight Templar, in regular standing.

2. It shall be the duty of the E. Commander to convene the Sir Knights of the Commandery, upon notice of the death of a Sir Knight, who may be entitled to receive funeral honors, upon request, made when living, or by his family after his decease, for the purpose of attending the funeral ceremonies.

3. Sir Knights, on such occasions, will attend in full uniform, pursuant to the regulations; their sword-hilts and the banner of the Commandery suitably dressed in mourning.

4. On the coffin of the deceased Sir Knight will be placed his hat and sword; and, if an officer, his jewel, trimmed with crape.

5. The E. Commander will preside during the services, and, assisted by the Prelate, lead in the ceremonies, pursuant to the Ritual. If Grand Officers or Past Grand Officers be present, they will be allotted a place in the procession according to their rank; and if the Grand Prelate or a Past Grand Prelate be present, he will take the place of the Prelate.

6. The Sir Knights will assemble at their Asylum, and march to the residence of the deceased, in the usual order of processions; the line being headed by the Warder, and the Officers being in the rear, according to

rank; that is, the E. Commander last; the Prelate being preceded by the Holy Writings, carried on a cushion, and the arms and hat of the deceased borne in the rear of the E. Commander. On arriving at the house, the lines are opened, and the E. Commander passes to the front, and receives the body, placing the hat and sword on the coffin, as above directed.

7. The procession is then formed as before; the body, with the mourners and citizens present, being in the rear of the Sir Knights, and in front of the Officers. If the services are performed at a church or place of public worship, the procession, on arriving, will enter in reversed order, the E. Commander and Prelate with the other Officers preceding the body and mourners.

8. When the public or religious services are concluded, the face of the deceased will be uncovered, and the Sir Knights (or a detachment of them) will form the "cross of steel" over the body, the E. Commander, with the Prelate, being at the head of the coffin, and the other Officers at the foot.

9. When more convenient or desirable, the part of the service, before going to the grave, as here indicated, may be performed at the house of the deceased, or be deferred till at the grave.

RITUAL.

E. Commander. SIR KNIGHTS: In the solemn rites of our Order we have often been reminded of the great truth, that we were born to die. Mortality has been brought to view, that we might more earnestly seek an immortality beyond this fleeting life, where death can come no more forever. The sad and mournful funeral knell has betokened that another spirit has winged its flight to a new state of existence. An alarm has come to the door of our Asylum, and the messenger was death; and none presumed to say to the awful presence: "Who dares approach?" A pilgrim warrior has been summoned, and "there is no discharge in that war." A burning taper of life, in our Commandery, has been extinguished, and none, save the High and Holy One, can re-light it. All that remains of our beloved Companion Sir Knight lies mute before us, and the light of the eye, and the breathing of the lips, in their language of fraternal greeting, have ceased for us forever, on this side of the grave. His sword, vowed only to be drawn in the cause of truth, justice and rational liberty, reposes still in its scabbard, and our arms can no more shield him from wrong and oppression.

The Sir Knights here return arms.

It is meet, at such a time, that we should be silent, and let the words of the Infinite and Undying speak, that we may gather consolation from His revelations, and impress upon our minds lessons of wisdom and instruction, and the meetness of preparation for the last great change which must pass upon us all.

Let us be reverently attentive while Sir Knight, our Prelate, reads to us a lesson from the Holy Scriptures.

Prelate. Help, Lord! for the faithful fail from among the children of men.

Response. Help us, oh Lord.

Prelate. The righteous cry, and the Lord heareth, and delivereth them out of all their troubles.

Response. Hear us, oh Lord.

Prelate. The Lord is nigh unto them that are of a broken heart, and saveth such as be of a contrite spirit.

Response. Be nigh unto us, oh Lord.

Prelate. The Lord redeemeth the soul of His servants; and none of them that trust in Him shall be desolate.

Response. Redeem us, oh Lord.

Prelate. For I will not trust in my bow, neither shall my sword save me.

Response. Redeem us, oh Lord.

Prelate. But God will redeem my soul from the power of the grave; for He shall receive me.

Response. Redeem us, oh Lord.

Prelate. Wilt Thou show wonders to the dead? Shall the dead arise and praise Thee? Shall Thy loving kindness be declared in the grave? or Thy faithfulness in destruction?

Response. Save us, oh Lord.

Prelate. We spend our days as a tale that is told. The days of our years are threescore years and ten; and, if by reason of strength, they be fourscore years, yet is their strength labor and sorrow, for it is soon cut off, and we fly away. So teach us to number our days, that we may apply our hearts unto wisdom.

Response. Teach us, oh Lord.

Prelate. For He knoweth our frame; He remembereth that we are dust. As for man, his days are as grass; as a flower of the field he flourisheth. For the wind passeth over it, and it is gone; and the place thereof shall know it no more. But the mercy of the Lord is from everlasting to everlasting upon them that fear Him.

Response. Show mercy, oh Lord.

Prelate. We shall not all sleep, but we shall all be changed; in a moment, in the twinkling of an eye, at the last trump; for the trumpet shall sound, and the dead shall be raised incorruptible, and we shall be changed. For this corruptible must put on incorruption, and this mortal must put on immortality. So when this corruption shall have put on incorruption, and this mortal shall have put on immortality, then shall be brought to pass the saying that is written, Death is swallowed up in victory. O death, where is thy sting? O grave, where is thy victory?

Response. O death, where is thy sting? O grave, where is thy victory?

Prelate. The sting of death is sin; and the strength of sin is the law. But thanks be to God, which giveth us the victory, through our Lord Jesus Christ.

Response. Thanks be to God.

E. Commander. Shall the memory of our departed brother fade from among men?

Response. It is cherished in our soul forever.

E. Commander. Shall no record be left of his virtues and worth?

Response. It is inscribed upon our hearts; it is written in our archives; the heart may cease to throb, and the archives may moulder and decay, but the tablets of the Recording Angel on high can never perish.

The Recorder here opens the Book of Records of the Commandery, on which a page is set apart, suitably inscribed, and says:

Thus it is written.

The Sir Knights uncover, and bow their heads.

E. Commander. He was a true and courteous Knight, and has fallen in life's struggle full knightly, with his armor on, prepared for knightly deeds.

Prelate. Rest to his ashes and peace to his soul.

Response. Rest to his ashes and peace to his soul.

Prelate. Sovereign Ruler of the Universe! into Thy hands we devoutly and submissively commit the departed spirit.

Response. Thy will be done, oh God.

The following Hymn will be sung:

Precious in the sight of Heaven
  Is the scene where Christians die;
Souls, with all their sins forgiven,
  To the courts of glory fly;
Every sorrow, every burden,
  Every Cross, they lay it down,
Jesus gives them richest guerdon,
  In his own immortal crown.

Here, above our brother weeping,
  Through our tears w e eize this hope:
He in Jesus sweetly sleeping,
  Shall awake to glory up.
He has borne his Cross in sorrow—
  Weary Pilgrim, all forlorn—
When the sun shines bright to-morrow
  'T will reveal his sparkling crown.

Knights of Christ! your ranks are broken!
  Close your front—the Foe is nigh!
Shield to shield, behold the Token,
  As he saw it in the sky!
By this sign, so bright, so glorious,
  You shall Conquer! if you strive;
And like him, though dead, victorious,
  In the sight of Jesus live.

The following Prayer will then be made by the Prelate; (or an extemporaneous Prayer may be made by him, or by any Clergyman present, as may be preferred):

Father of Lights! In this dark and trying hour of calamity and sorrow, we humbly lift our hearts to Thee. Give us, we pray, that light which cometh down from above. Thou hast mercifully said, in Thy holy word, that the bruised reed Thou wouldst not break; remember in mercy, oh Lord, before Thee. [Be Thou, at this hour, the Father of the fatherless, and the widow's God. Administer to them the consolations which they so sorely need.] Cause us to look away from these sad scenes of frail mortality, to the hopes which lie beyond the grave, and bind us yet closer together in the ties of brotherly love and affection. While we see how frail is man, and how uncertain the continuance of our lives upon the earth, and are reminded of our own mortality, lead us, by Thy grace and spirit, to turn our thoughts to those things which make for our everlasting peace; and give us a frame of mind to make a proper improvement of all the admonitions of Thy providence, and fix our thoughts more devotedly on Thee, the only sure refuge in time of need. And at last, when our earthly pilgrimage shall be ended, "when the silver cord shall be loosed, and the golden bowl be broken," oh wilt Thou, in that moment of mortal extremity, be indeed *Immanuel* —Christ with us; may "the lamp of Thy love" dispel the gloom of the dark valley, and we be enabled, by the commendations of Thy Son, to gain admission into the blessed Asylum above; and, in Thy glorious presence, amidst its ineffable mysteries, enjoy a union with the spirits of the departed, perfect as is the happiness of heaven, and durable as the eternity of God. *Amen.*

Response. Amen, and Amen, and Amen.

The procession will then form and march to the place of interment, in the same order as before.

On arriving at the place, while forming in order, a suitable Dirge or the following Hymn may be sung:

AIR—*Pleyel's Hymn.*

Softly, sadly bear him forth,
To his dark and silent bed;
Weep not that he's lost to earth,
Weep not that his spirit's fled.

By our trials, hope and fear;
By our anguish keenly felt;
Let us trust God will be near,
When we're at His altar knelt.

This, our brother, gone before,
May we in remembrance keep,
Hoping, as time passes o'er,
We shall meet where none e'er weep.

Sadly now we leave his form,
In the tomb to moulder still;
Hoping, in th' eternal morn,
Christ His promise will fulfill.

One last look—one parting sigh;
Ah, too sad for words to tell;
Yet, tho' tears now dim each eye,
Hope we still, and sigh, farewell!

On reaching the grave, the Sir Knights will form a triangle around it, the base being at the foot, the E. Commander and Prelate being at the head, and the friends and relatives at the foot, and the service will thus proceed:

Prelate. SIR KNIGHTS: There is one sacred spot upon the earth where the footfalls of our march are unheeded; our trumpets quicken no pulse, and incite no fear; the rustling of our banners and the gleam of our swords awaken no emotion—it is the silent city of the dead, where we now stand. Awe rests upon every heart, and the stern warrior's eyes are bedewed with feelings which never shame his manhood. It needs no siege, nor assault, nor beleaguering host to enter its walls; we fear no sortie, and listen for no battle-shout. No Warder's challenge greets the ear, nor do we wait awhile with patience for permission to enter.

Hither must we all come at last; and the stoutest heart and the manliest form that surrounds me will then be led a captive, without title or rank, in the chains of mortality and the habiliments of slavery, to the King of Terrors.

But if he has been faithful to the Captain of his salvation, a true soldier of the Cross; if he has offered suitable gifts at the shrine of his departed Lord, and bears the signet of the Lion of the tribe of Judah, then may he claim to be of that princely house, and to be admitted to audience with the Sovereign Master of Heaven and Earth. Then will he be stripped of the chains of earthly captivity, and clothed in a white garment, glistening as the sun, and be seated with princes and rulers, and partake of a libation, not of death and sorrow, but of that wine which is drank forever new in the Father's kingdom above.

We cannot come here without subdued hearts and softened affections. Often as the challenge comes which takes from our side some loved associate, some cherished companion in arms, and often as the trumpet sounds its wailing notes to summon us to the death-bed, and the brink of the sepulchre, we cannot contemplate "the last of earth" unmoved. Each successive death-note snaps some fibre which binds us to this lower existence, and makes us pause and reflect upon that dark and gloomy chamber where we must all terminate our pilgrimage. Well will it be for our peace then, if we can wash our hands, not only in token of sincerity, but of every guilty stain, and give honest and satisfactory answers to the questions required.

The sad and solemn scene now before us stirs up these recollections with a force and vivid power which we have hitherto unfelt. He who now slumbers in that last, long, unbroken sleep of death, was our brother. With him have we walked the pilgrimage of life, and kept ward and watch together in its vicissitudes and trials. He is now removed beyond the effect of our praise or censure: That we loved him, our presence here evinces, and we remember him in scenes to which the world was not witness, and where the better feelings of humanity were exhibited without disguise. That he had faults, and foibles, is but to repeat what his mortality demonstrates—that he had a human nature, not divine. Over these errors, whatever they may have been, we cast, while living, the mantle of charity; it should, with much more reason, enshroud him in death. We, who have been taught to extend the point of charity, even to a foe, when fallen, cannot be severe or merciless toward a loved brother.

The memories of his virtues lingers in our remembrance, and reflects its shining lustre beyond the portals of the tomb. The earthen vase which has contained precious odors will lose none of its fragrance, though the clay be broken and shattered. So be it with our brother's memory.

The Junior Warden then removes the sword and hat from the coffin, which last will then be lowered into the grave, while the Prelate relates as follows:

Prelate. "I am the resurrection, and the life: he that believeth in me, though he were dead, yet shall he live; and whosoever liveth, and believeth in me, shall never die." To the earth we commit the mortal remains of our deceased brother, as we have already commended his soul to his Creator, with humble submission to Divine Providence. (*Here cast some earth on the coffin.*) Earth to earth; (*here cast again,*) ashes to ashes; (*here cast more earth,*) dust to dust; till the morn of the resurrection, when, like our arisen and ascended Redeemer, he will break the bonds of death, and abide the judgment of the great day. Till then, friend, brother, Sir Knight, Farewell! Light be the ashes upon thee, and "may the sunshine of Heaven beam bright on thy waking!"

Response. Amen, and Amen, and Amen!

The Junior Warden then presents the sword to the E. Commander, who says:

E. Commander. Our departed brother Sir Knight was taught, while living, that this sword in his hands, as a true and courteous Knight, was endowed with three most estimable qualities: its hilt with *fortitude* undaunted; its blade with *justice* impartial; and its point with *mercy* unrestrained. To this lesson, with its deep emblematical significance, we trust he gave wise heed. He could never grasp it without being reminded of the lively significance of the attributes it inculcated. He has borne the pangs of dissolving nature —may we trust that it was with the same *fortitude* that he sustained the trials of this passing existence; to his name and memory be *justice* done, as we hope to receive the like meed ourselves; and may that *mercy*, unrestrained, which is the glorious attribute of the Son of God, interpose in his behalf to blunt the sword of Divine Justice, and admit him to the blessed companionship of saints and angels in the realms of light and life.

Response. Amen, and Amen, and Amen!

The Senior Warden then presents a Cross to the Prelate, who says:

Prelate. This symbol of faith—the Christian's hope and the Christian's faith—we again place upon the breast of our brother, there to remain till the last trumpet shall sound, and earth and sea yield up their dead. Though it may, in the past history of our race, have been perverted at times into an ensign of oppression, and crime, and wrong; though it may have been made the emblem of fraud, and superstition, and moral darkness, yet its significance still remains as the badge of the Christian warrior. It calls to mind Gethsemane and its sorrowful garden; the judgment-hall of Pilate, and the pitiless crown of thorns; Golgotha and Calvary, and their untold agonies, that fallen man might live and inherit everlasting life. If an inspired Apostle was not ashamed of the Cross, neither should we be; if he gloried in the significance of the truths it shadowed forth, so ought we to rejoice in it as the speaking witness of our reliance beyond the grave. May this hope of the living have been the anchor to the soul of our departed brother—the token to admit him to that peaceful haven "where the wicked cease from troubling and the weary are at rest."

Response. Amen, and Amen, and Amen.

The Prelate then casts the Cross into the grave, and continues:

Prelate. The orders of the Christian Knighthood were instituted in a dark period of the world's history, but their mission was high and holy. To succor and protect the sorrowing and destitute, the innocent and oppressed, was their vow and their life-long labor and duty. For long, long years they well and nobly performed their vows and did their devoirs. In those rude ages the steel blade was oftener the arbiter of justice, than the judgments of judicial tribunals or the decrees of magistrates. So long as the Templars adhered to their vows of poverty, they were virtuous and innocent, and their language was, in truth, "Silver and gold have I none, but such as I have, give I unto thee." But, with the accession of wealth and civil power, they were tempted, and fell from their high estate, and their possessions attracted the cupidity, and their prowess incurred the hatred of the despots of those times. When the martyred DeMolay had perished, and the order was proscribed, they united with the fraternity of Free and Accepted Masons, and returned to their primitive simplicity of manners, and a rough habit, coarse diet, and severe duty, was all that was offered to their votaries.

In our land, we have perpetuated only the distinctive rights, with the appellations and regulations of the defenders of the Holy Sepulchre—the early champions and soldiers of the Cross—and this as a guerdon of merit, not a badge of rank. The sword in our hands is more as a symbol of the duties we are vowed to fulfill, than as an instrument of assault or defense. We claim to exercise practical virtues in the holy bonds of our confraternity, in humble imitation of those renowned knights of the olden time; for there is still in this refined age innocence to be guarded, widowed hearts to be relieved of their burdens, and orphanage to be protected from the chill blasts of a wintry world. And to be true and courteous is not limited to any age or clime.

Our brother, whose cold and lifeless remains have just been committed to the earth, was one of our fraternal band, bound by the same ties and pledged to the same duties. To his bereaved and mourning friends and relatives we have but little worldly consolation to offer, but we do tender to them our heartfelt sympathies. And if the solemn and interesting ceremonies in which we have been engaged, have not pointed to them a higher hope and a better consolation, then all our condolence would be in vain.

Sir Knight companions, let us pray:

ALMIGHTY and most merciful God! we adore Thee as the Sovereign Ruler of all events, both in time and for eternity. As it hath pleased Thee to take from our ranks one dear to our hearts, we beseech Thee to bless and sanctify unto us this dispensation of Thy providence. Inspire our hearts with wisdom from on high, that we may glorify Thee in all our ways. May we have Thy divine assistance, oh, most merciful God! to redeem our misspent time; and in the discharge of the important duties Thou hast assigned us in our moral welfare here below, may we be guided by faith and humility, courage and constancy, to perform our allotted pilgrimage acceptable in Thy sight, without asking a remission of years from Thee. And when our career on earth is finished, and the sepulchre appointed for all the living receives our mortal bodies, may our souls, disengaged from their cumbrous dust, flourish and bloom in eternal day, and enjoy that rest which Thou hast prepared for Thy good and faithful servants in Thy blessed Asylum of peace beyond the vails of earth. All which we ask through the mediation of our Redeemer, King of kings, and Lord of lords. *Amen*

Response. Amen, and Amen, and Amen.

E. Commander. Attention, Sir Knights!

The lines are then formed, and the cross of steel made over the grave, and the following Hymn is sung:

AIR—*Mount Vernon.*

Christian warriors at the pealing
  Of the solemn vesper bell,
Round the tri-form altar kneeling,
  Whisper, each, "IMMANUEL!"

When the watch and ward are over,
  Guarding the Asylum well,
Smiles of peace around them hover,
  At Thy name, IMMANUEL!

When the matin-notes are ringing,
  Cheerfully from mount and dell,
Strength for warfare still is springing
  From Thy name, IMMANUEL!

When some deed of emprise sharing,
  Deed like those traditions tell,
Prompts each Knight to noble daring—
  'Tis for Thee, IMMANUEL!

When the storm-clouds darkly lower
  On our pathway dark and fell,
Knight heroic will not cower,
  Cheered by Thee, IMMANUEL!

When death's fearful damps are stealing,
  And is breathed the last "Farewell!"
All the brighter world revealing,
  Thou shalt come, IMMANUEL!

The Sir Knights may then escort the friends of the deceased to their home, or return to their Asylum, as may be expedient.

DIRGE.

Angels! roll the rock away!
Death yield up thy mighty prey!
See! He rises from the tomb,
Rises with ımmortal bloom.

'Tis the Saviour—Seraphs, raise
Your triumphant shouts of praise;
Let the earth's remotest bound
Hear the joy-inspiring sound.

Lift, ye saints—lift up your eyes!
Now to glory see Him rise!
Hosts of angels on the road,
Hail and sing th' incarnate God.

Heaven unfolds its portals wide:
Gracious conquerer, through them ride,
King of Glory! mount Thy throne,
Boundless empire is Thine own.

Praise him, all ye heavenly choirs,
Praise, and sweep your golded lyres;
Praise him in the noblest songs;
Praise him with ten thousand tongues.

TEMPLAR'S SONG.

As when the weary trav'ler gains
  The height of some commanding hill,
His heart revives, if o'er the plains
  He sees his home, though distant still;

So, when the Christian pilgrim views
  By faith his mansion in the skies,
The sight his fainting strength renews,
  And wings his speed to reach the prize.

The hope of heaven his spirit cheers;
  No more he grieves for sorrows past;
Nor any future conflict fears,
  So he may safe arrive at last.

O Lord, on Thee our hopes we stay,
  To lead us on to Thine abode;
Assur'd Thy love will far o'erpay
  The hardest labors of the road.

ODE.

MUSIC—"Sweet Home."

Farewell, till again we shall welcome the time
Which brings us once more to our fame-cherished shrine;
And though from each other we distant may roam,
Again may all meet in this our dear lov'd home.
    Home, home—sweet, sweet home.
May every dear brother find joy and peace at home.

And when our last parting on earth shall draw nigh,
And we shall be called to the Grand Lodge on high,
May each be prepared when the summons shall come,
To meet the Grand Master in Heaven our home.
    Home, home—sweet, sweet home.
May every dear brother find Heaven a home.

www.ingramcontent.com/pod-product-compliance
Lightning Source LLC
LaVergne TN
LVHW011143110826
845150LV00008B/2487

* 9 7 8 1 4 1 8 1 9 2 8 1 5 *